Welcome

Name:

Contact:

Cover by Patt Legge

Printed in the United States of America

First Printing, 2018

Book ISBN: 9781718155145

Disclaimer

This workbook makes no representation or warranty of any kind (express, implied or statutory) in relation to this workbook or anything made available on or through this workbook, including but not limited to website, programs, products, services, opt-in gifts, e-books, videos, webinars, blog posts, e-newsletters, consultations, e-mails, social media and/or other communication (collectively referred to as "Website"), excludes (to the extent permitted by applicable law) all such warranties. You are agreeing to accept all parts of this Disclaimer. Thus, if you do not agree to the Disclaimer below. Please stop and do not access or use this content.

The content contained on this workbook is provided for general information only. Any advice or information received through this workbook or its content should not be relied upon as being correct or accurate. It is your obligation to verify independently such matters from primary sources of information and by taking specific professional advice. You must not rely on the content or associated service of this workbook to do this for you.

By using this workbook, you agree to absolve me of any liability or loss that you or any other person may incur from use of the information, products or materials that you request or receive through or on my workbook. You agree that I will not be liable to you, or to any other individual, company or entity, for any type of damages, including direct, indirect, special, incidental, equitable or consequential loss or damages, for use of or reliance on my workbook. You agree that I do not assume liability for accidents, delays, injuries, harm, loss, damage, death, lost profits, personal or business interruptions, misapplication of information, physical or mental disease or condition or the issue, or any other type of loss or damage due to any act or default by me or anyone acting as our agent, consultant, affiliate, joint venture partner, employee, shareholder, director, staff, team member, or anyone otherwise affiliated with my business or me, who is engaged in delivering content on or through this workbook.

This workbook provides references or links for your convenience to the information, opinions, advice, programs, products or services of any other individual, business or entity and do not necessarily endorse the material on these sites. In the event you purchase or obtain goods or services from a third party then your acquisition of such goods or services will be in accordance with the third party's terms and conditions and this workbook will have no liability to you in respect of the same. I am not responsible for the website content, blogs, e-mails, videos, social media, programs, products and/or services of any other person, business or entity that may be linked or referenced in my workbook. Conversely, should my workbook link appear in any other individual's, business's or entity's website, program, product or services, it does not constitute my formal endorsement of them, their business or their website and other content either.

All materials on this site are protected by copyright and intellectual property laws and are the property of Patt Legge. Unless stated otherwise, all materials for personal, classroom or library, non-commercial use.

Notes to parents

Handwriting skill is important for all kids, it's an essential tool for communicate to the world. Without this skill kids will lose an important presenting tool for their future learning and working. And the goal of this workbook is to develope thier tracing skill from line to shape and then letters.

You can help kid's handwriting by
1) Lead your kid take it slow, line by line. Explain when mistakes happen.
2) Make sure kid hold pencil in right positioned, which is called a tripod grasp.
3) Beware kid's hand stregth to write, it can develope by let kid play clay and play dough.

A Tripod Grasp Pencil Holding:
1) Place forefinger on top of the pencil working with thumb for most of control.

2) Rest pencil on the middle finger for support and accuracy tracing.

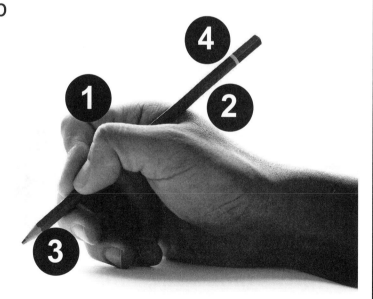

3) Rest pencil base between thumb and forefinger near the base of the thumb.

4) Keeping the pencil at a 45 degree angle positioned.

Notes to kids

Tracing follow the dashed line.

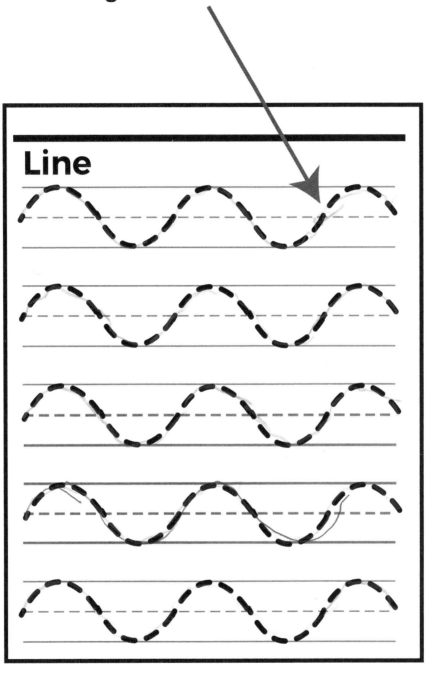

Line

Line

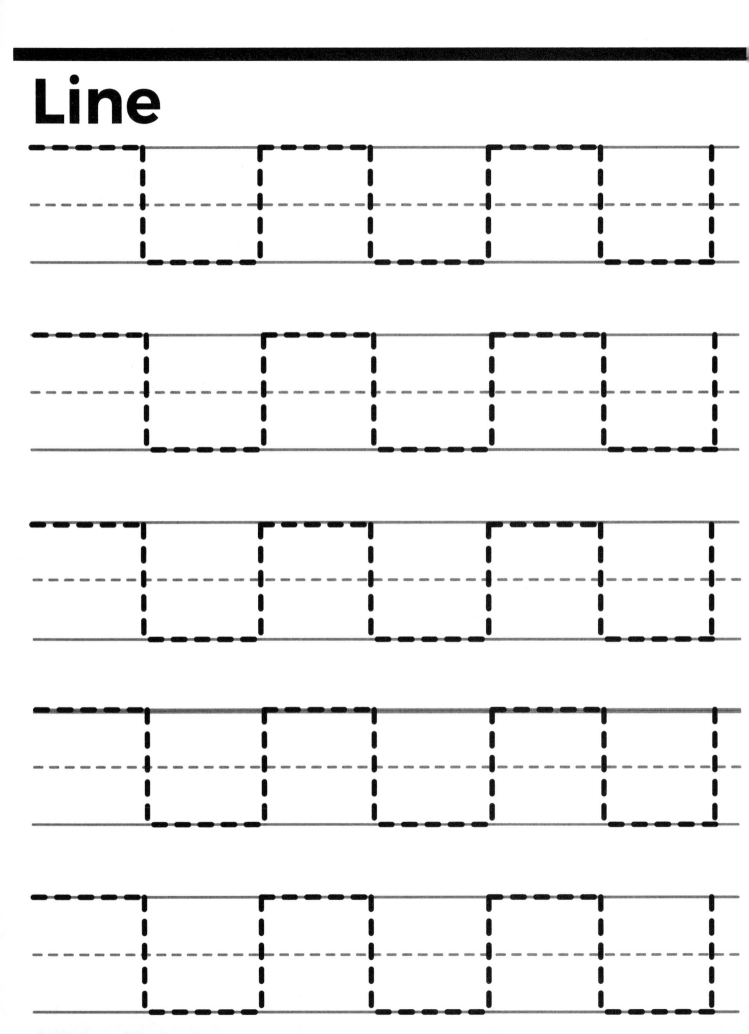

Line

Line

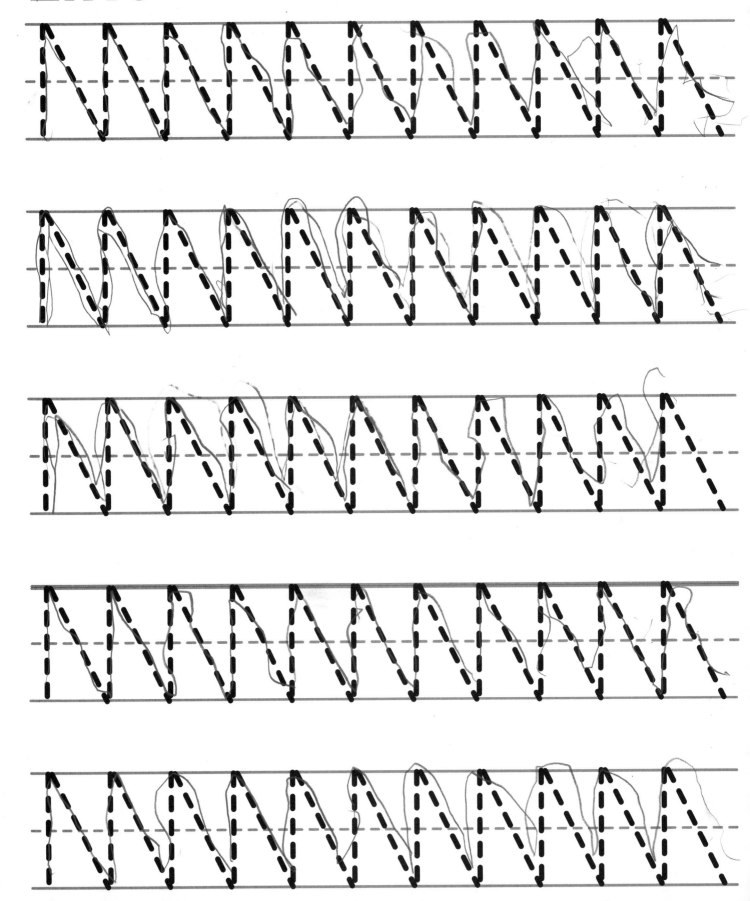

Line

Line

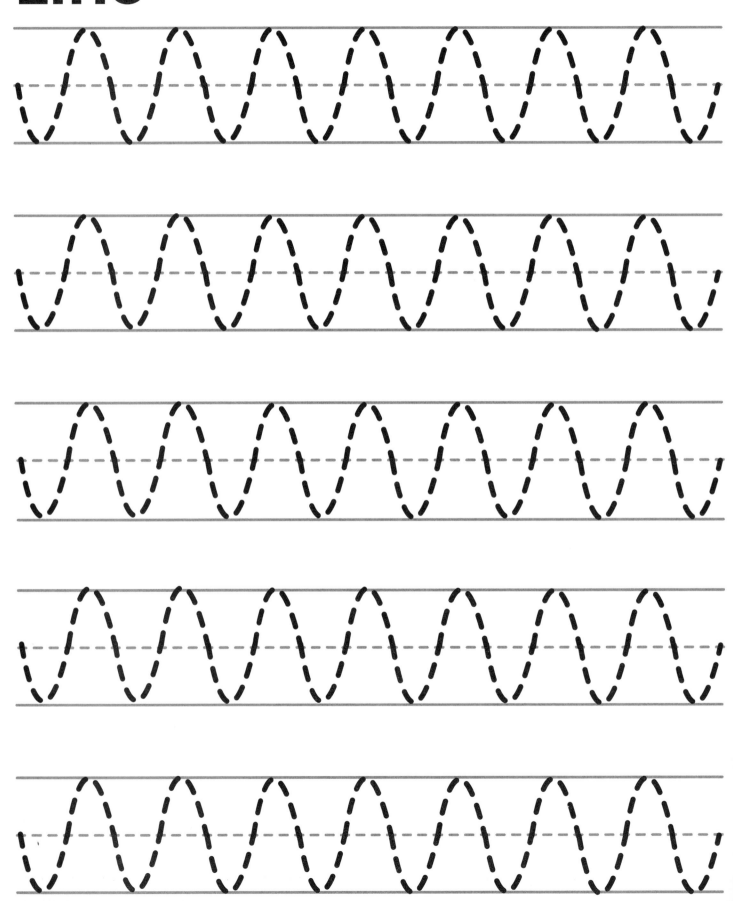

Notes to kids

**Tracing follow the dashed line.
To finish the shape**

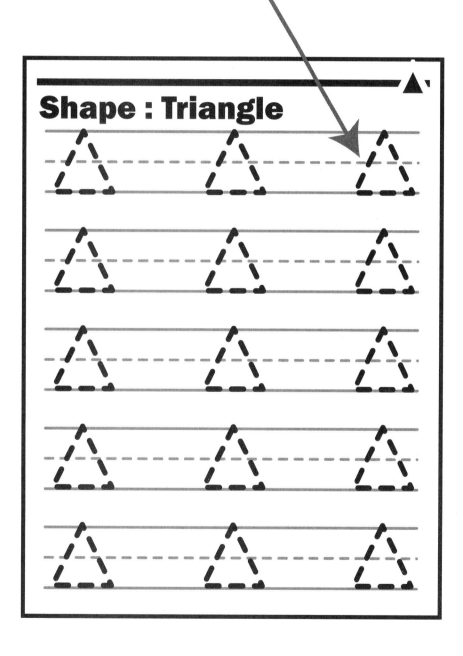

Shape : Circle

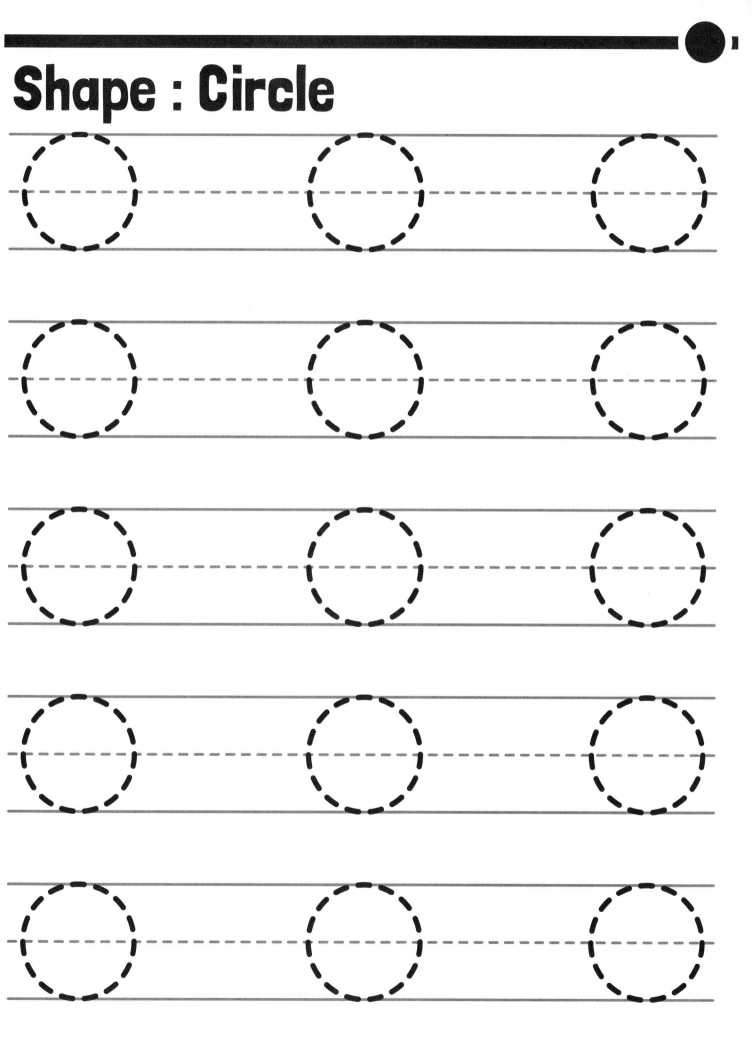

Shape : Triangle

Shape : Square

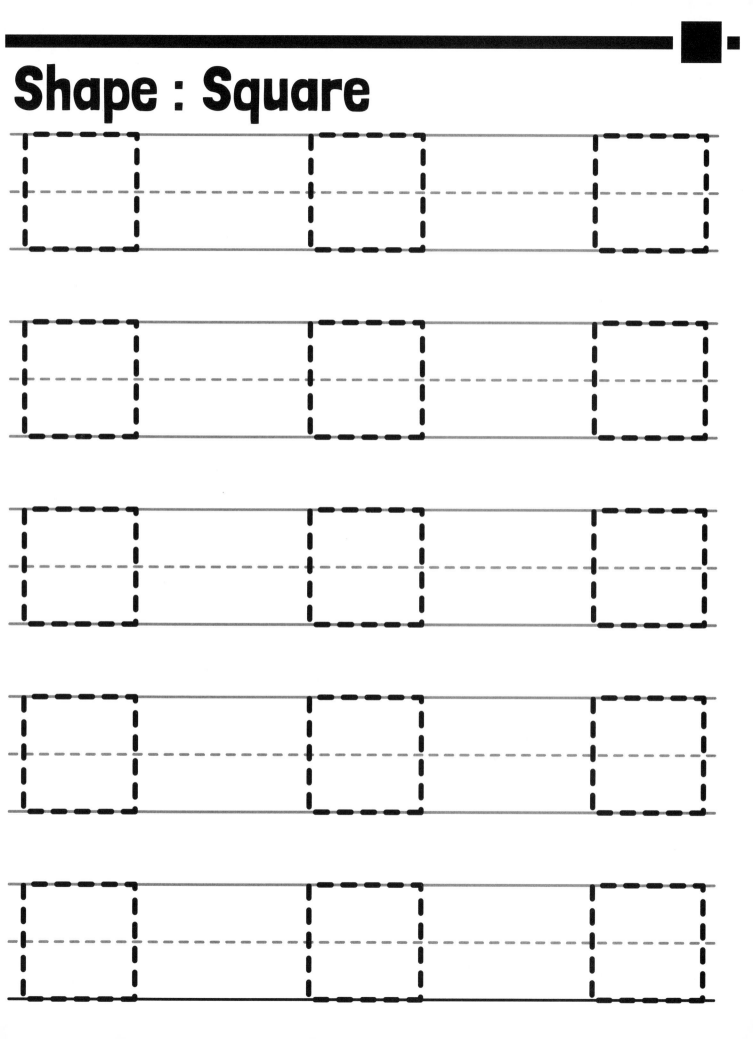

Shape : Star

Shape : Moon

Shape : Trapezoid

Shape : Pentagon

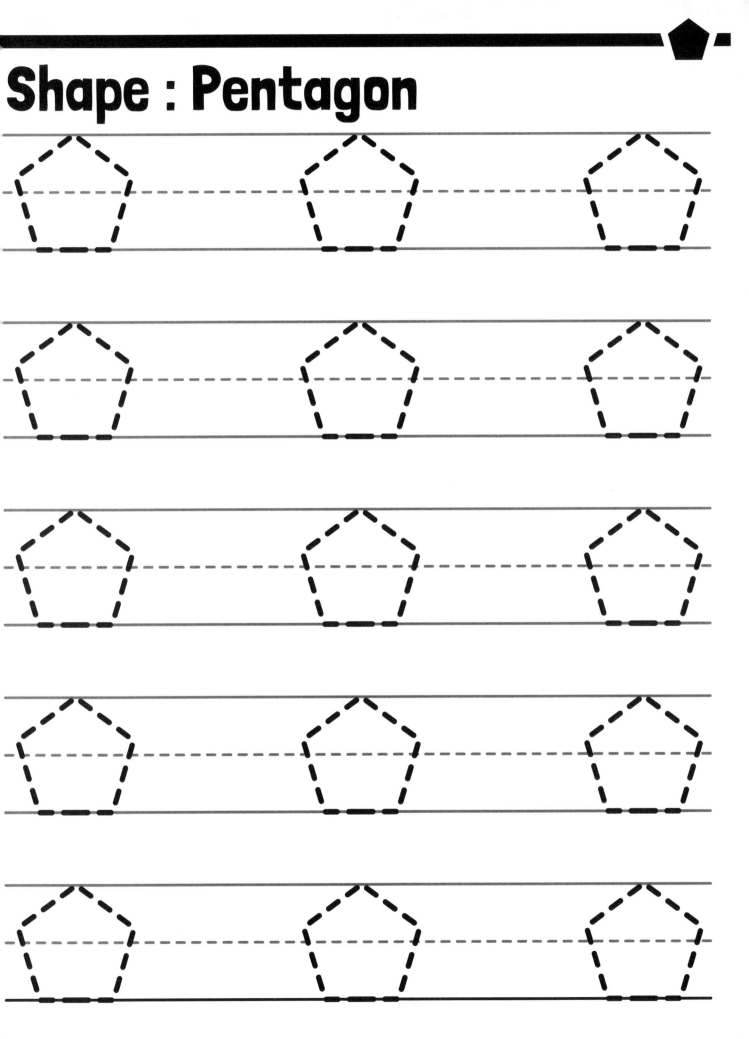

Shape : Hexagon

Shape : Octagon

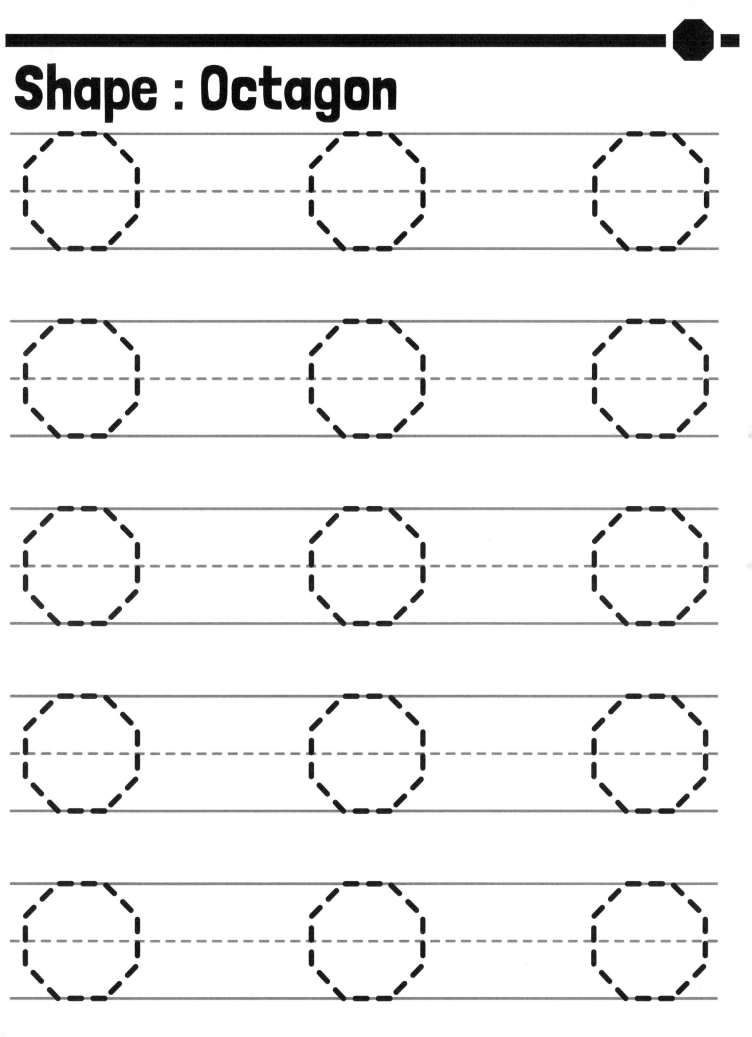

Shape : Diamond

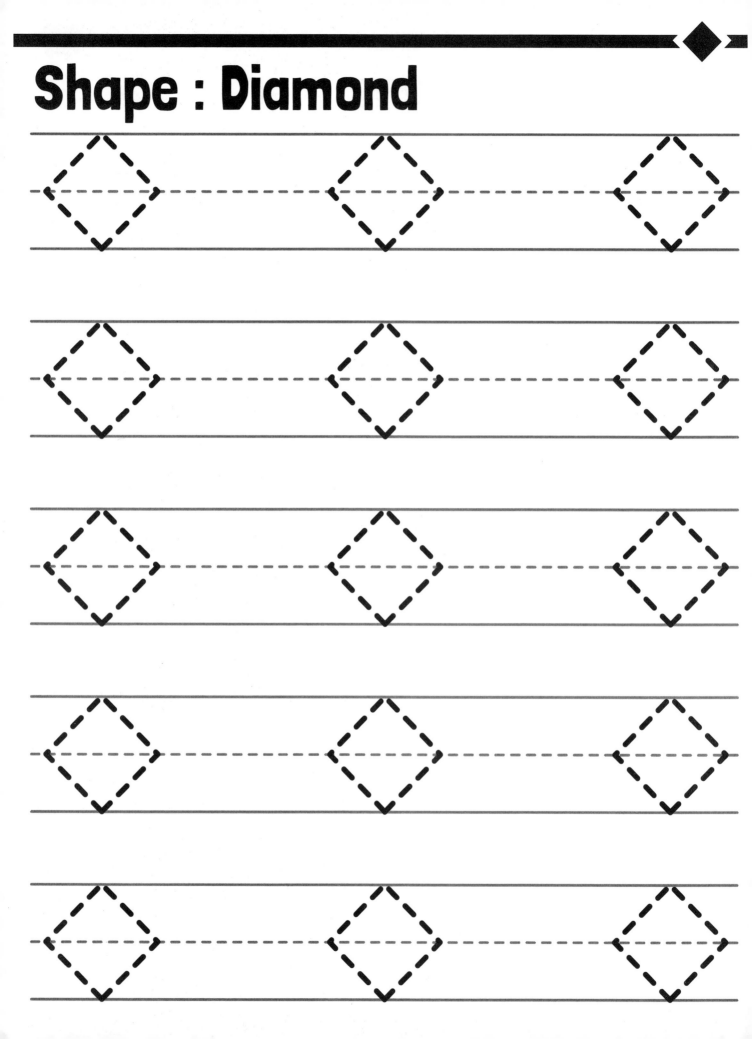

Shape : Parallelogram

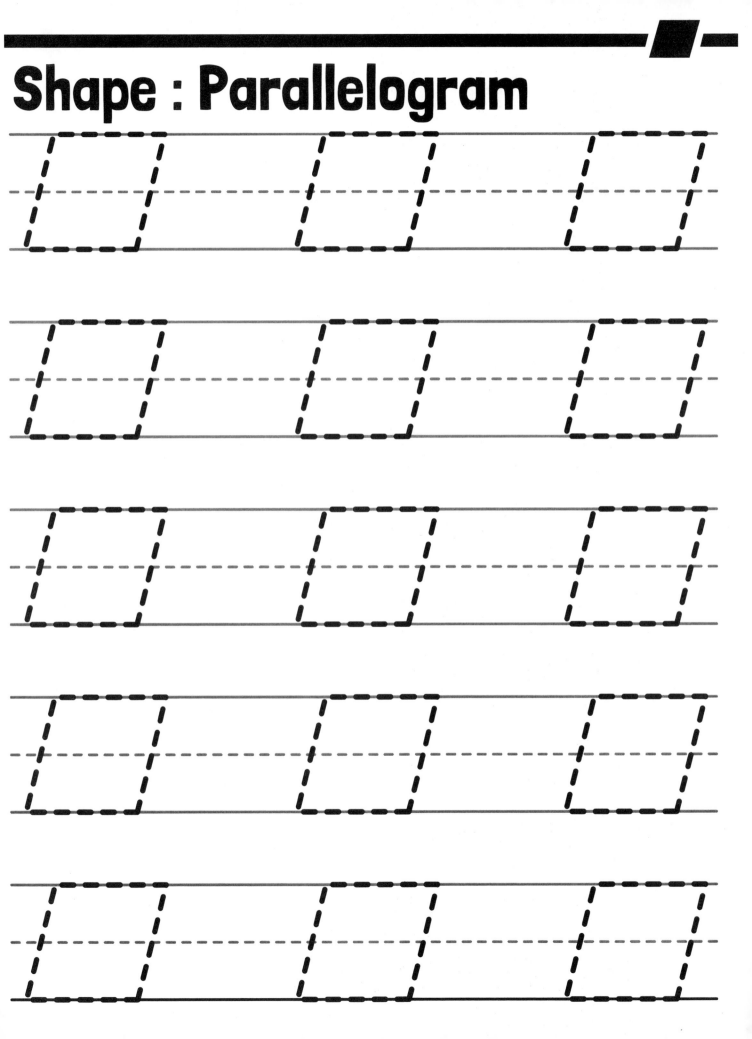

Shape : Arrow

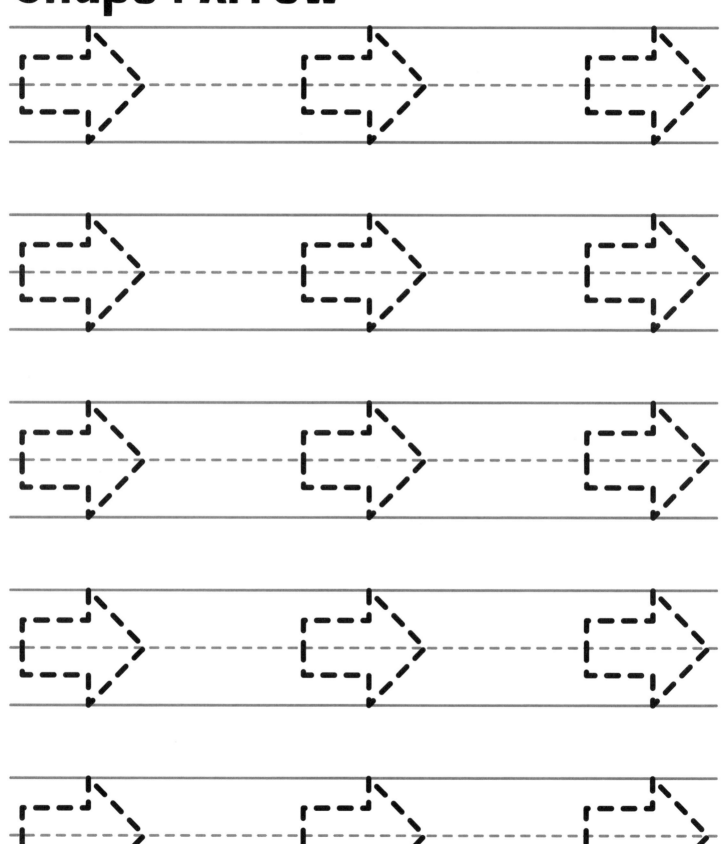

Notes to kids

Tracing follow the dashed line.
To finish the letter

Color it.

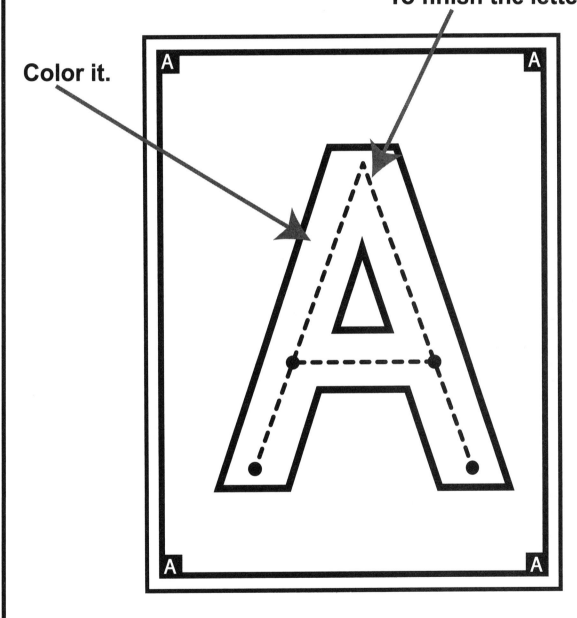

A A

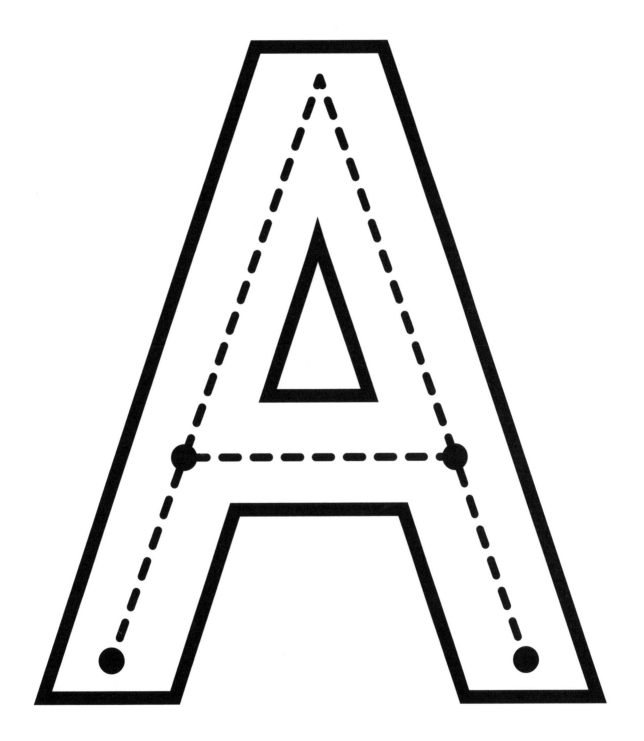

A A

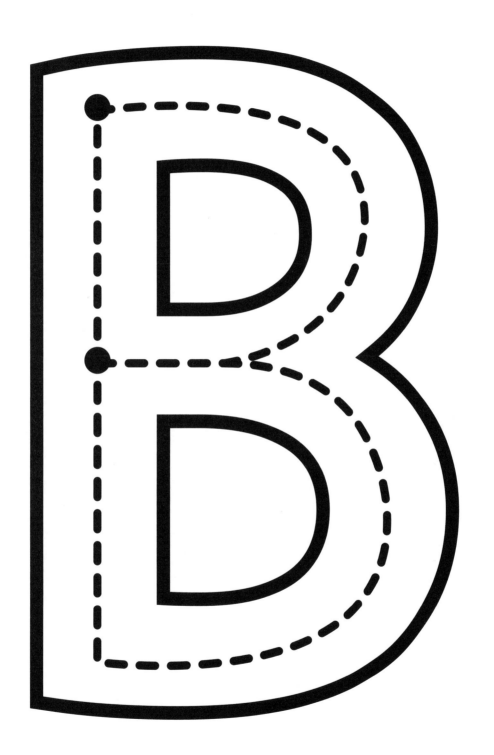

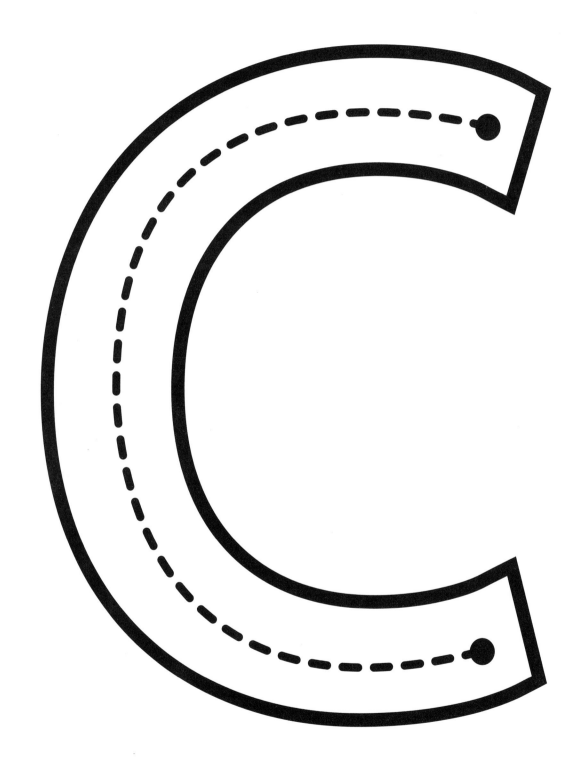

D D

D

D D

E

E

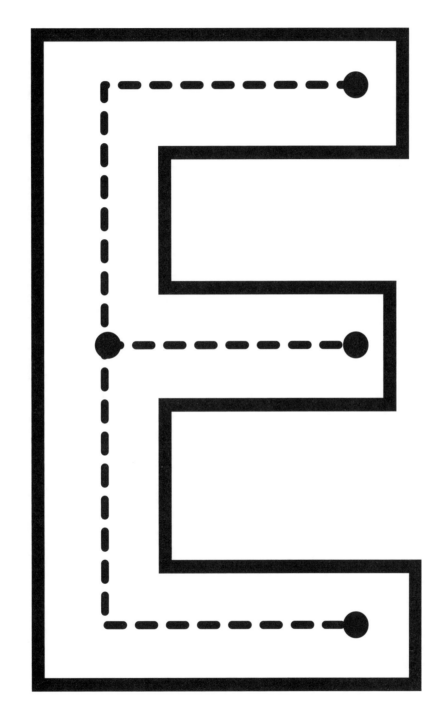

E

E

F F

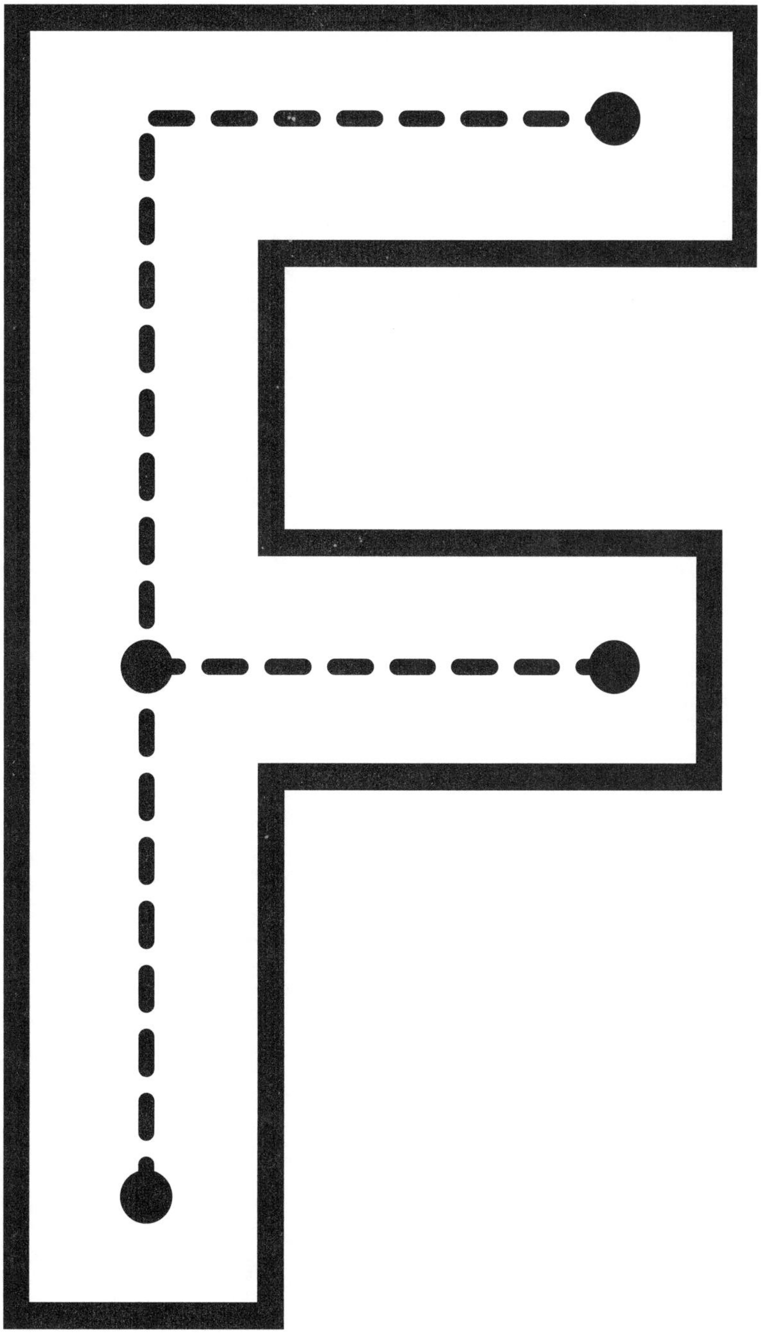

F F

G G

G G

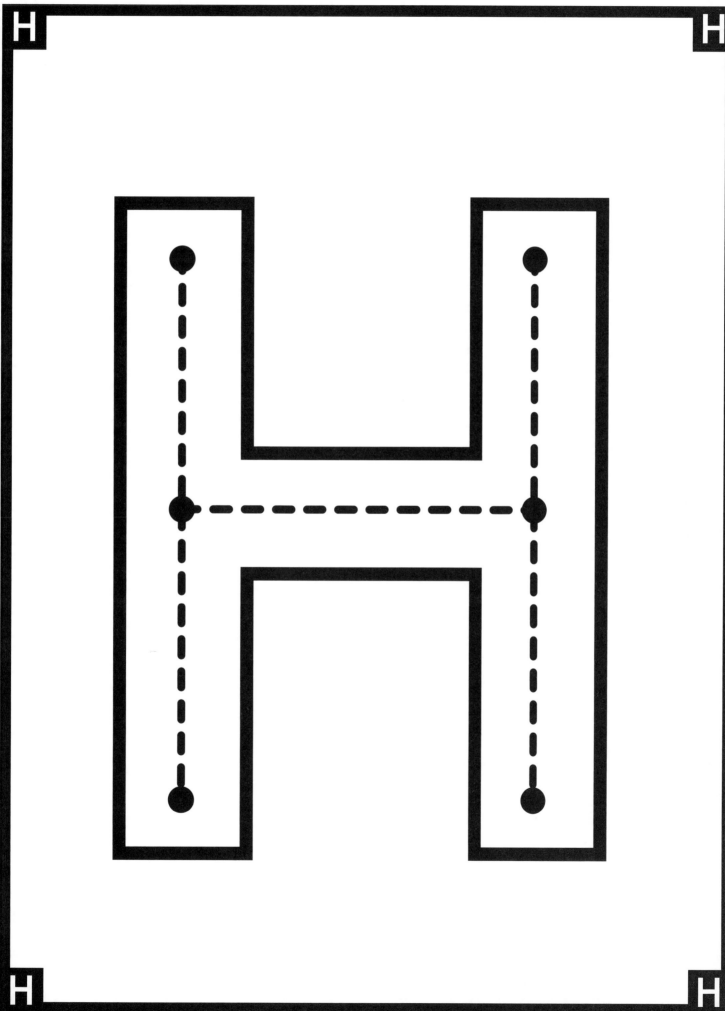

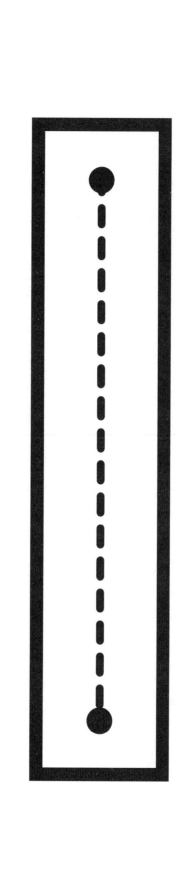

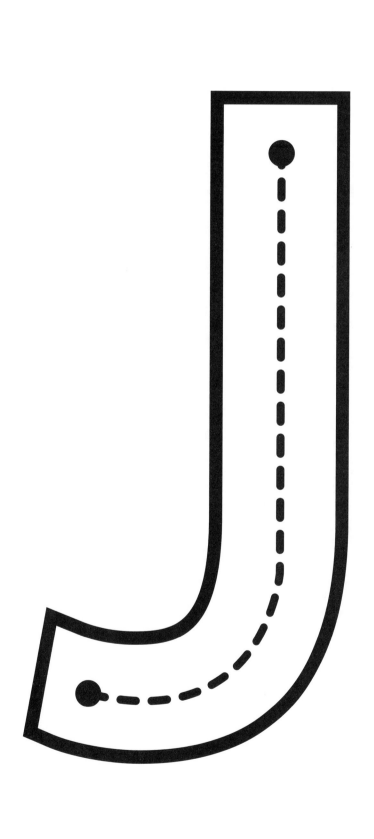

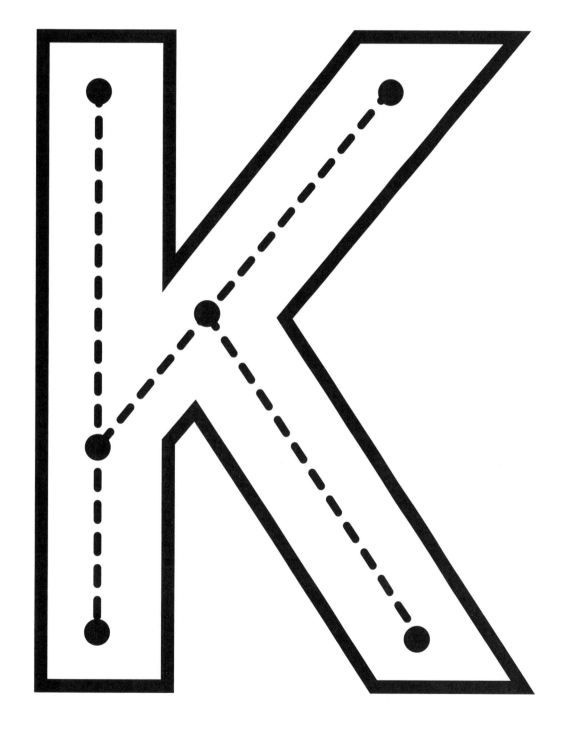

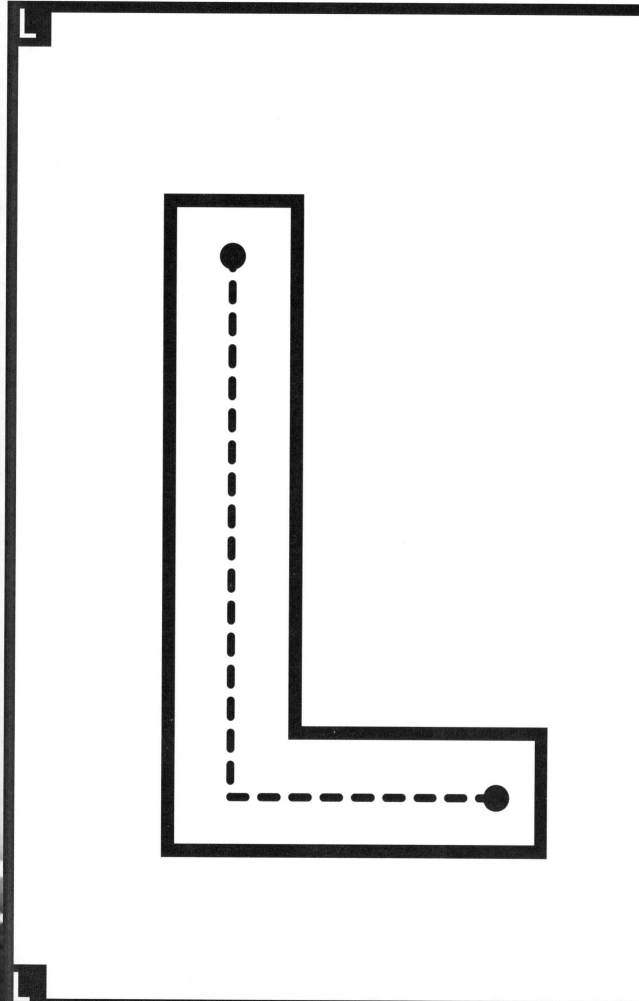

M

M

M

M

N

N

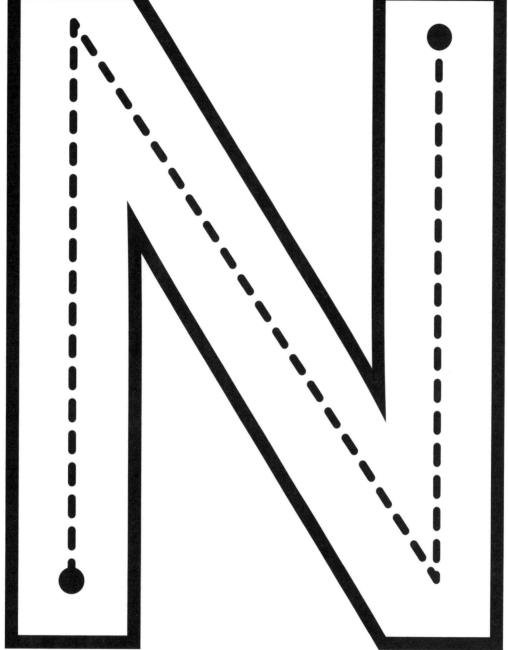

N

N

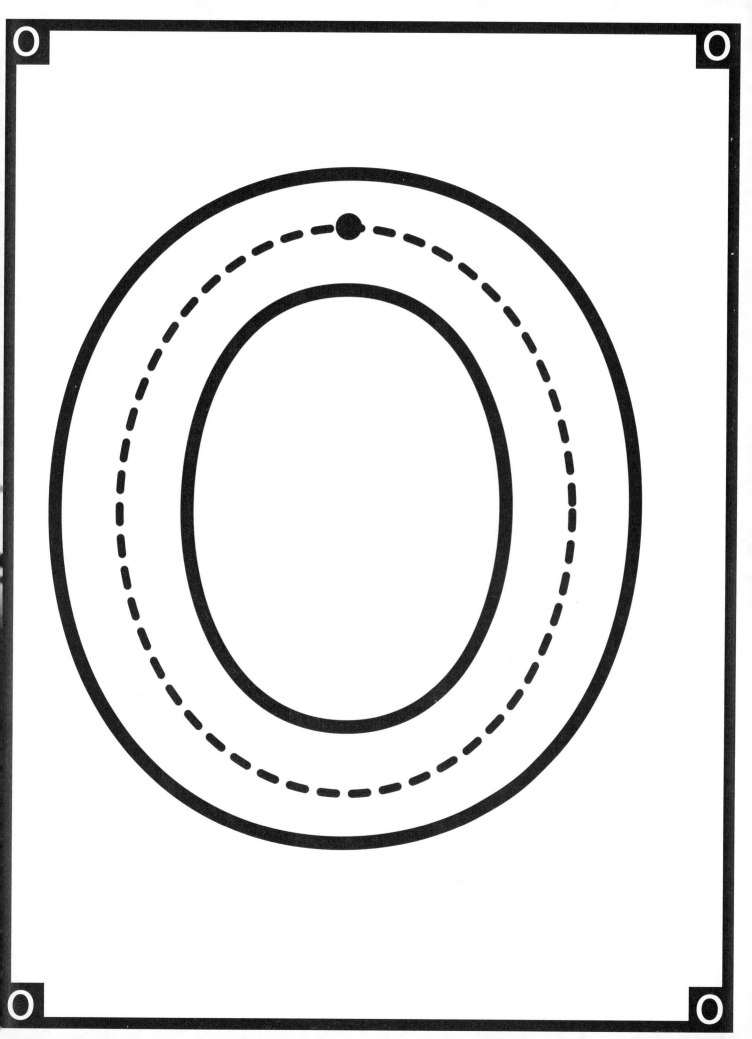

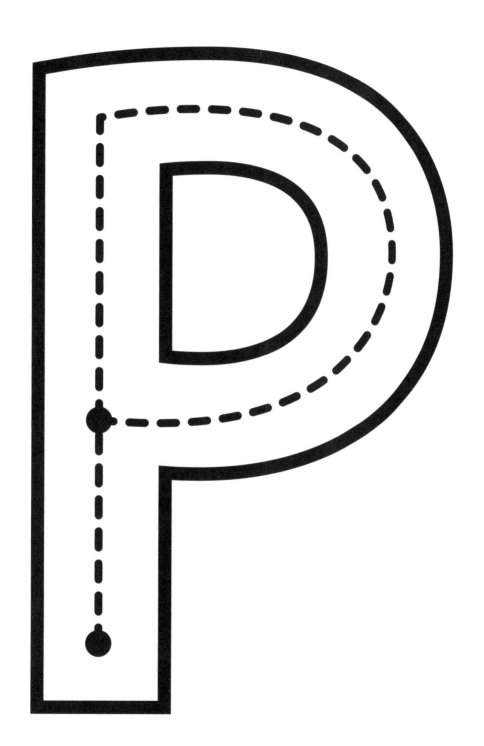

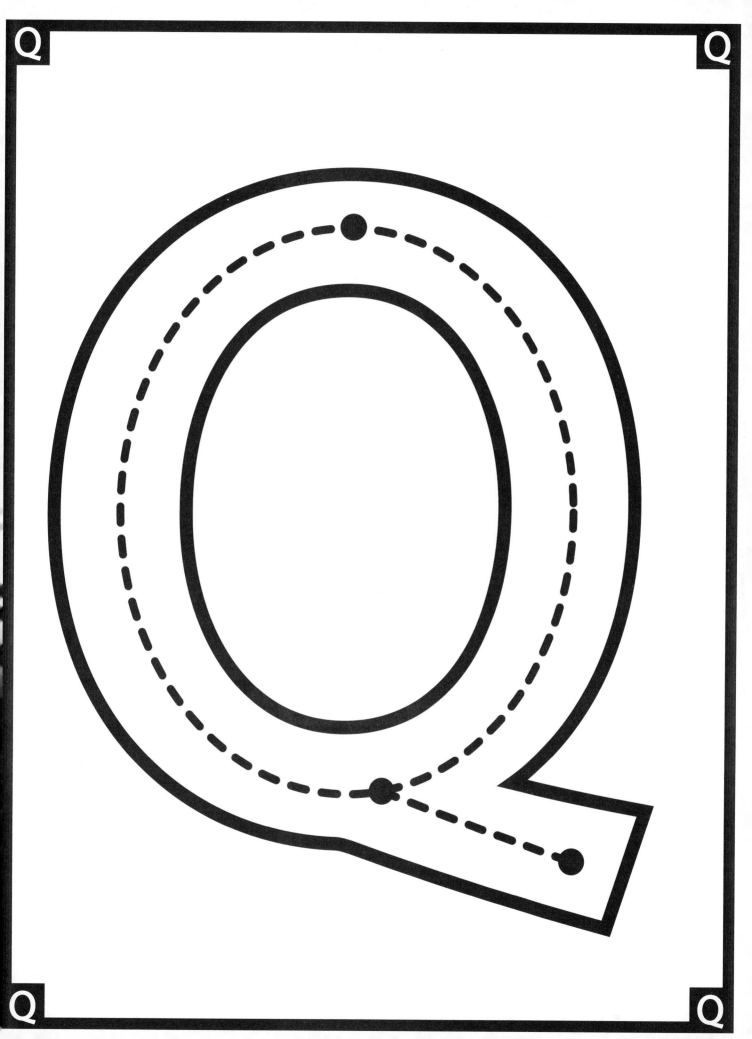

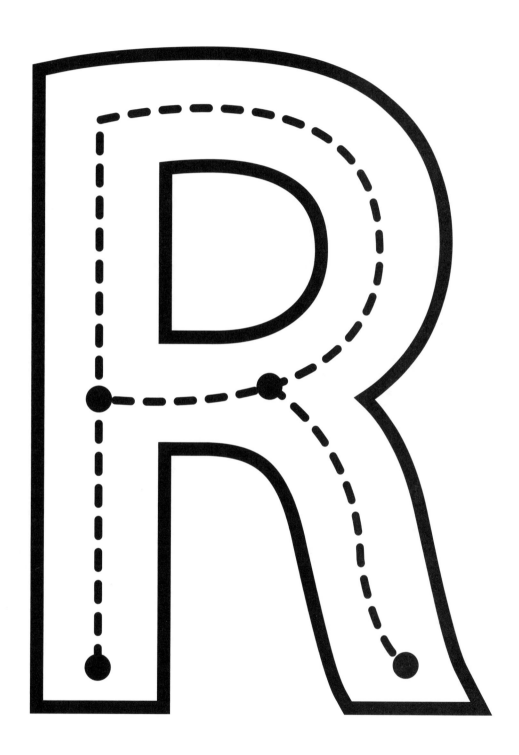

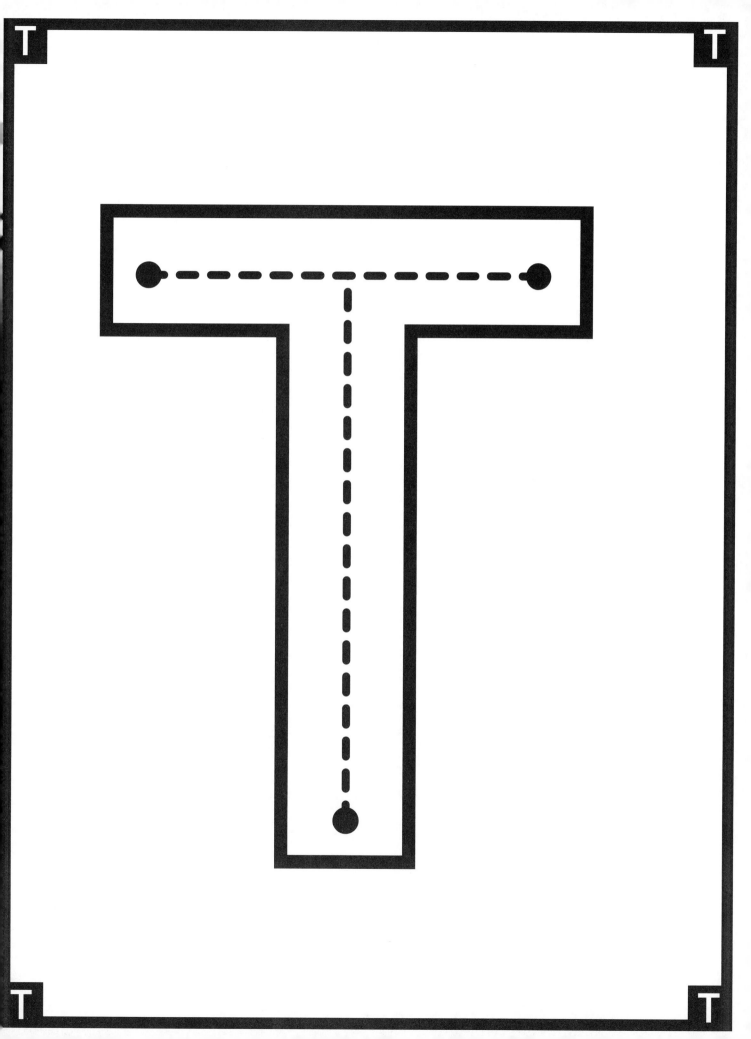

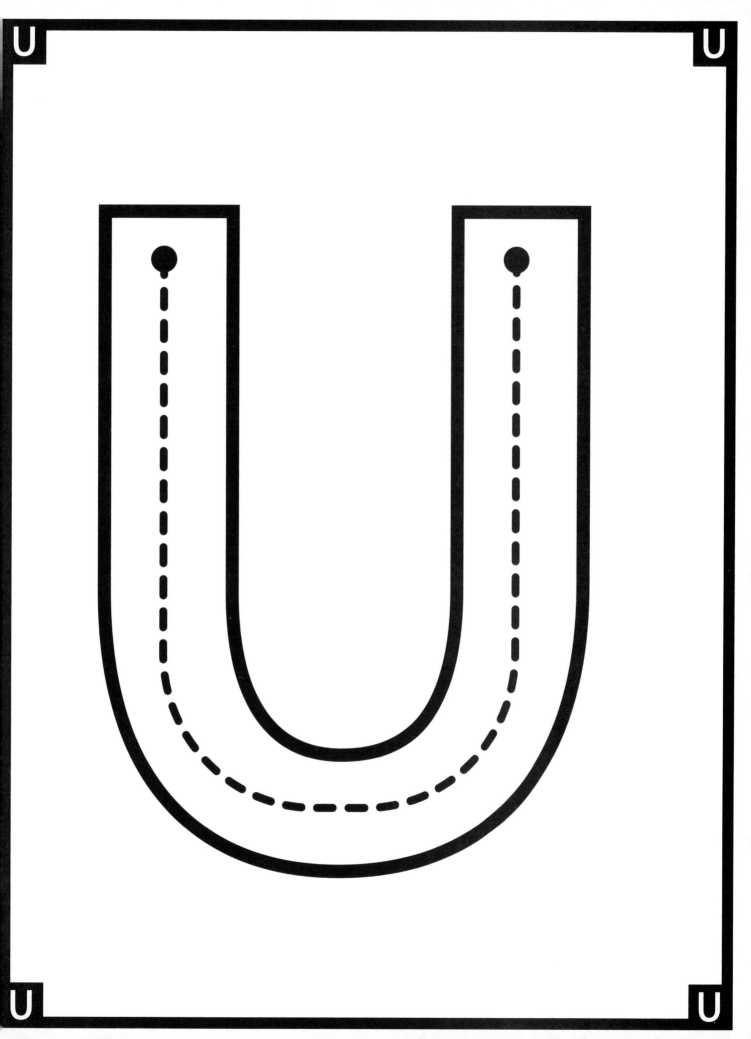

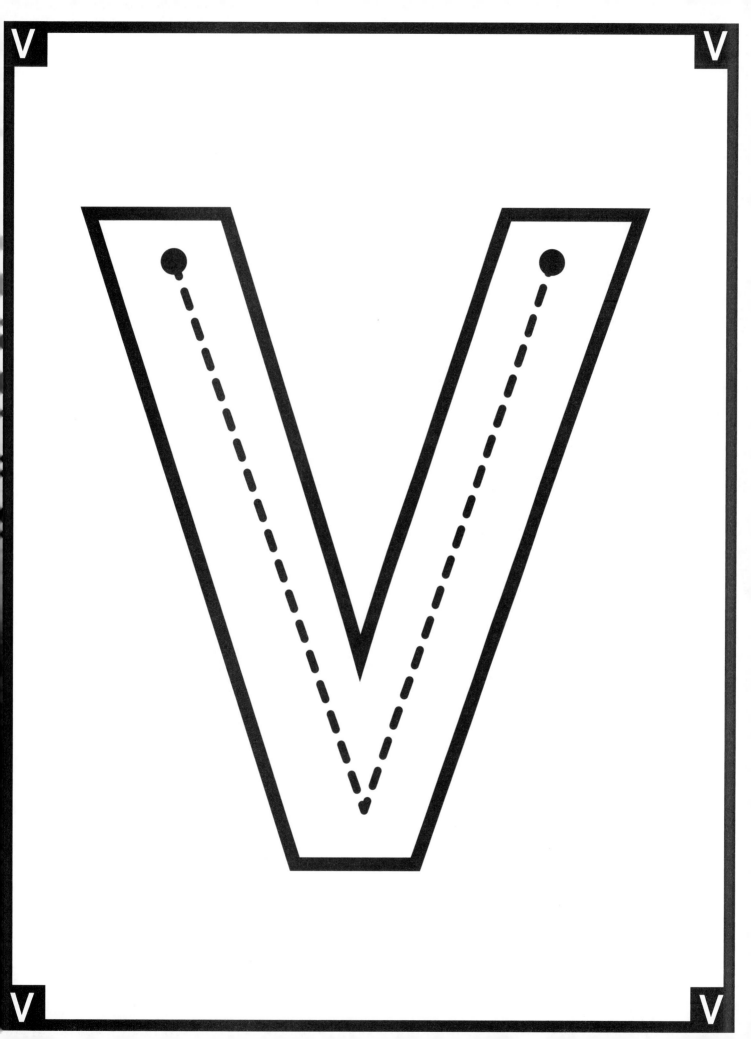

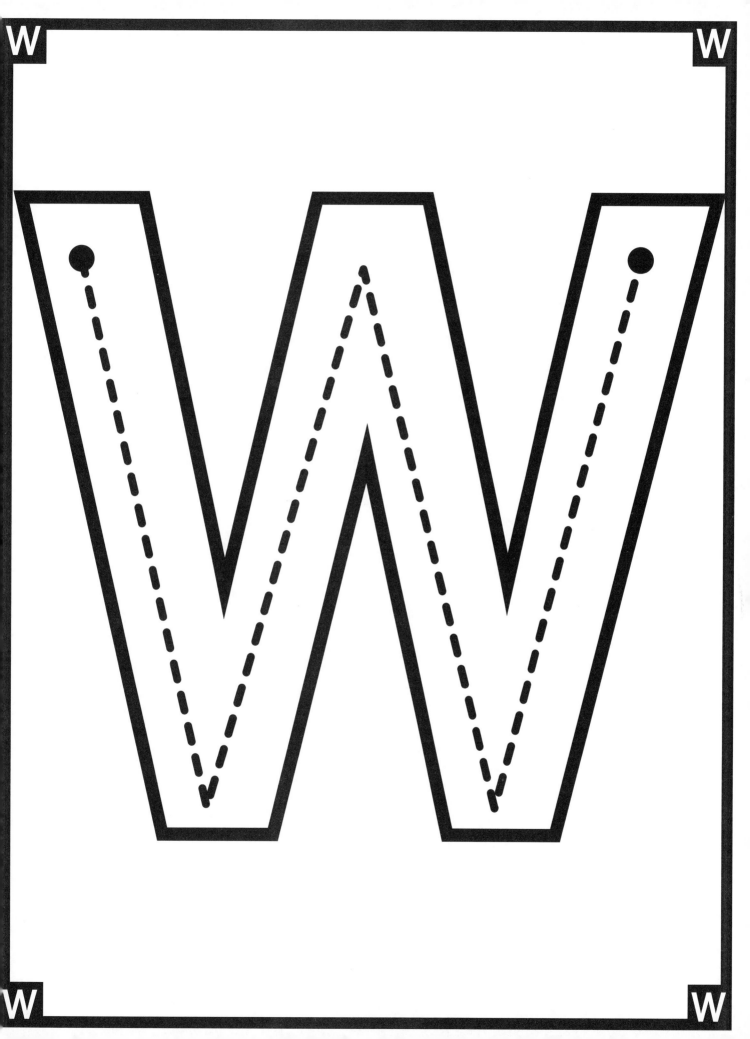

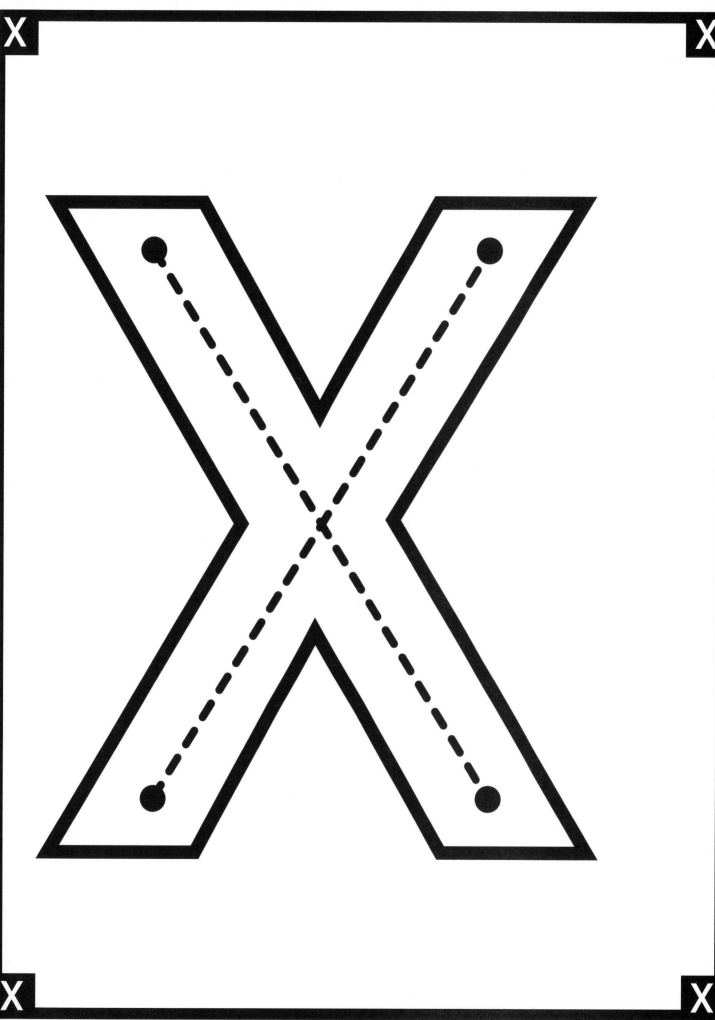

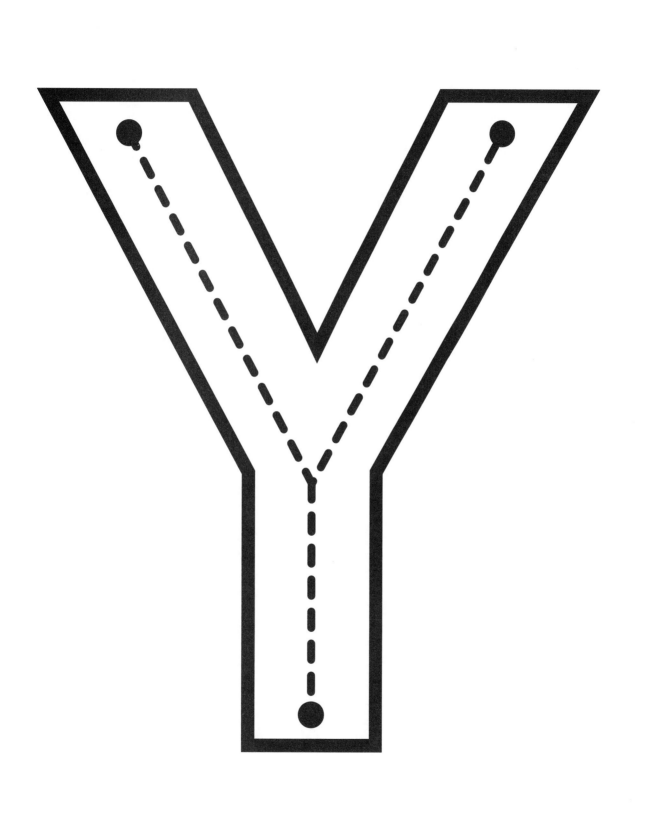

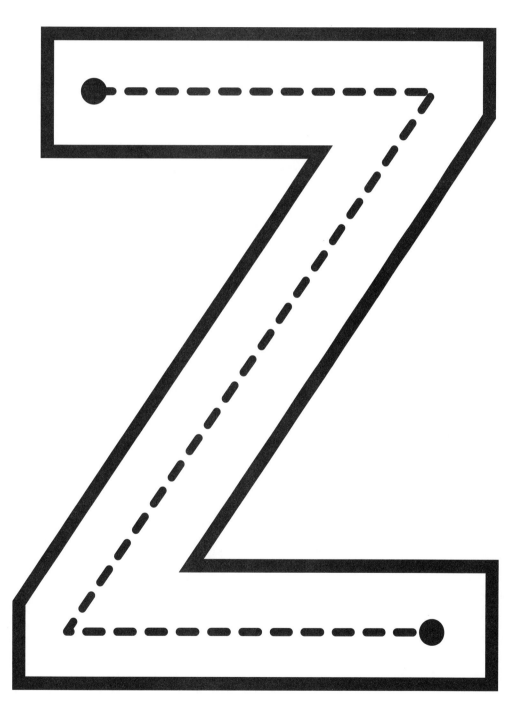